The Words of King Lemuel

The Virtuous Woman of Proverbs 31

James Daughtry

Abidan

Published by Abidan
Bridgeview, IL 60455
www.abidanbooks.com

All Scripture verses from The Holy Bible: King James Version

ISBN-13: 978-0-9850371-2-3
ISBN-10: 0-9850371-2-1

Library of Congress Control Number: 2020911920

To my wife Claudia, a virtuous woman.

Contents

Introduction

As a young man, I wondered what I should look for in a wife. When I asked an older Christian man who was happily married, he told me to read Proverbs 31. He assured me that the Proverb would teach me everything I needed to know. My adrenaline raced and I could not wait to get home to read it! After reading the Proverb, however, I was disappointed and confused. The words seemed antiquated, the illustrations outdated, and it made little sense to me. Nevertheless, I thought that I needed to understand this Proverb. Therefore, I asked some young ladies that I knew about the Proverb assuming they would be able to shed some light on it for me. When I asked them, they laughed and said things like, "Oh, you mean Superwoman" or "that Proverb is unrealistic, the woman never sleeps." Their answers left me even more confused and made me wonder whether the Bible would have an example of a virtuous woman that is not realistic.

My doubts and confusion led me down a long road of research and investigation. As I studied the customs of the ancient Middle East and the Hebrew language, I gained a deeper insight into this amazing Proverb. Since King Lemuel wrote these words thousands of years ago, people in modern times often struggle to make sense of them. Yet once his words are understood, the hidden truths are clearly revealed. When I began to comprehend the meaning of his words, I discovered a treasure of wisdom and knowledge. One thing I realized is that the Proverb is not just about a virtuous woman but about life in general. Proverbs 31 has made me reflect on many areas of life and is one of the passages in the Bible that has impacted me the most.

This book contains two keys for unlocking the secrets of King Lemuel's teaching. The first key is a careful examination of some of the Hebrew words. Their origin and significance provide insights to interpreting the Proverb. The second key is a study of the lifestyle of the people of that time period. Their customs and culture reveal many clues into the valuable lessons in this Proverb.

In each chapter of this book, you will learn of an ancient land and civilization. Although their way of life was different, similarities exist between their society and ours. As you embark on this journey into the past, try to forget our modern world and imagine theirs.

Chapter 1

A Mother's Advice

Proverbs 31:1-2
1 The words of king Lemuel,
the prophecy that his mother taught him.
2 What, my son? and what, the son of my womb?
and what, the son of my vows?

For centuries, people have pondered the words of King Lemuel. Some have even attempted to learn more about him. However, the only ancient manuscript that mentions King Lemuel is Proverbs 31. Many questions exist as to who he was, but the answers have been lost to history. Yet men and women can still learn timeless truths from his beautiful and mysterious words.

Often, people think that Proverbs 31 was written by a demanding man who thought that women should serve men. However, one of the first things that King Lemuel states is fascinating.

In verse 1, who taught the King these words?

The words written by King Lemuel were actually taught to him by a woman, his mother, who wanted the best for her son. She most likely began instructing him on the themes in this Proverb from his youth. When he was young, her words were probably gentle, but as he grew older, she may have had to firmly lecture him. The Hebrew word translated as "taught" has the idea of both instruction and correction.[1]

Although his mother most likely had many talks with him, King Lemuel vividly remembers this one. Maybe he was starting to go down the wrong path. Possibly he was entering manhood. Perhaps he was about to take the throne. Whatever the case, his mother felt that she needed to speak with him. King Lemuel probably wrote this Proverb many years later. He could have been an older man, but still able to clearly recall this occasion and his mother's profound words. Obviously, this particular talk was firmly etched in his memory.

In the second verse, the mother of King Lemuel communicates her deep love and concern for him. She uses the word "son" three times apparently to get his attention and emphasize her point. She lets him know that she carried him in her womb and he is her biological son. King Lemuel's mother also uses this opportunity to talk to him about spiritual things. She tells him that he is the son of her vows which is a testimony to God's work in her life and his. She does not give the reason why she made vows. Perhaps she had trouble conceiving or had a difficult pregnancy. Whatever the case, King Lemuel's mother expressed that she cared for him and that he is her son by the grace of God. As she shares these words with him, her passion and emotion are evident.

Proverbs 31:3-5
3 Give not thy strength unto women,
nor thy ways to that which destroyeth kings.
4 It is not for kings, O Lemuel, it is not for kings
to drink wine; nor for princes strong drink:
5 Lest they drink, and forget the law,
and pervert the judgment of any of the afflicted.

The mother of King Lemuel knew that men are sometimes led astray by their desires. Some men spend their time, money, and energy on women that are not of good character. In verse 3, King Lemuel's mother firmly warns him not to fall into this trap. In addition, she mentions something in verses 4-5 that has been a snare to men for centuries.

What is her warning to him in verses 4-5?

_____

King Lemuel's mother was concerned that her son would be tempted by alcohol. Kings often held royal feasts and drinking was common. Also, the stress of ruling the kingdom could have tempted him to turn to alcohol. His mother's warning was for his own good as well as the good of others. He had the responsibility not only of his household, but the entire nation.

Proverbs 31:6-9
6 Give strong drink unto him that is ready to perish,
and wine unto those that be of heavy hearts.
7 Let him drink, and forget his poverty,
and remember his misery no more.
8 Open thy mouth for the dumb in the cause
of all such as are appointed to destruction.
9 Open thy mouth, judge righteously,
and plead the cause of the poor and needy.

The identity of King Lemuel's mother is also a mystery. Her name is not mentioned and no information is given about her. However, one thing is clear. She wanted to teach her son to be wise and instill in him a genuine concern for people. She specifically points out people that he should not neglect.

Who does she mention in verses 6-9?

_____

_____

People often help others who later may be able to help them. King Lemuel's mother instructs him to help people who probably would never be able to do anything for him in return. She teaches him to have true compassion and not do things for ulterior motives.

When people study the virtuous woman of this Proverb, they usually overlook verses 1-9 and focus on verses 10-31. However, the first nine verses help us to better understand King Lemuel, his mother, and the virtuous woman.

How would you describe the mother of King Lemuel based on verses 1-9?

King Lemuel's mother understood many of the struggles and temptations that men face. She also knew that there were virtuous women and not so virtuous women. Although her words appear to end in verse 9, she surely must have taught her son about the qualities of a virtuous woman. It has been said that only a woman can understand another woman. The famous words of King Lemuel about a virtuous woman in verses 10-31 were undoubtedly influenced by his mother's teaching. He beautifully wrote these verses in the form of a poem. One feature that can only be observed in Hebrew is that he starts each verse with a letter of the Hebrew alphabet. This feature makes the verses easy to remember and since he used the whole alphabet, it shows a full consideration of the topic. He also may have put the verses to music. Jewish people have sung them for generations as a way to praise and honor women.[2, 3]

King Lemuel may not have understood his mother's counsel in the beginning. This is often the case when a mother or father tries to give instruction to their child. Although children may not always understand or obey the instruction of their parents, they do hear their words. Often when children are older, they will remember and appreciate the teaching of their parents. This Proverb shows that a mother's words to her child were not forgotten!

Write any additional thoughts you have on verses 1-9.

_____

_____

Chapter 2

A Virtuous Woman

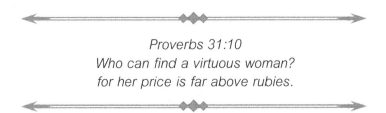

Proverbs 31:10
Who can find a virtuous woman?
for her price is far above rubies.

King Lemuel begins his teaching on the virtuous woman with a question that people have long contemplated. Some think he is saying that finding a virtuous woman would be an extremely difficult task. Others believe he is suggesting that a virtuous woman does not exist.

What are your thoughts on his question?

_____

_____

Although his question may be puzzling, it serves an important purpose. The question draws attention to the value of a virtuous woman. His statement afterward confirms this as he exclaims, "her price is far above rubies." The question also raises other important questions such as: What is a virtuous woman and who can be one?

What do you think makes a woman virtuous?

_____

_____

The word "virtuous" is a translation of the Hebrew word "chayil" which is normally used to describe men. Therefore, the meaning is a little difficult to understand when used with a woman. In general, the Hebrew word has the idea of force and this woman truly was a force in her family and community. Usually, the word refers to physical strength, but it can also refer to inner strength. Sometimes the word can even refer to financial strength or wealth. Often, the word refers to a mighty army or a valiant soldier. Perhaps King Lemuel is suggesting that this woman was a warrior, not in the military sense, but in her love and passion for life and for others. A woman will obviously manifest "chayil" in different ways than a man. As you study this book, you will learn about the strengths, abilities, and character of this virtuous warrior.[1,2,3]

Many people feel that no woman could ever compare to the virtuous woman of Proverbs 31. Since the Proverb is considered a poem, some people claim that she is fictional. However, much of the Bible was written in poetic form yet based on real events. King Lemuel and his mother surely knew virtuous women. The detailed description of a virtuous woman in this Proverb certainly came from real life observations.

Every woman has the potential to be virtuous. Some women may already be virtuous. Others may be a diamond in the rough and with a little polishing their brilliance will be revealed. For others, they may need some rough edges removed before they can be polished and shine. Sadly, some women might be on the entirely wrong path and need a complete turnaround in their life.

What do you think keeps a woman from being virtuous?

_____

_____

The Hebrew word in this verse translated "woman" is from the same root word that God used in Genesis when He created woman. Although the woman in this Proverb is married, single women can be virtuous as well. Every woman has opportunities to love and serve others. King Lemuel provides principles in this Proverb that can be applied by all women. In addition, he wrote these words to provide instruction for men. At the end of the Proverb, he actually gives a command that is directed to everyone. Therefore, his teaching is clearly for all to heed and obey.

Chapter 3

A Confident Husband

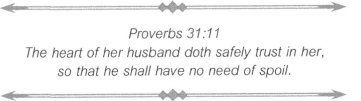

Proverbs 31:11
The heart of her husband doth safely trust in her,
so that he shall have no need of spoil.

The virtuous woman has a positive impact on a wide range of people as King Lemuel will reveal in this Proverb. He starts, however, with the positive impact that she has on her husband. The virtuous woman has fully gained his trust. She has proven to him that she is responsible and dependable. The husband has complete confidence in her judgment and abilities.

King Lemuel begins the story of the virtuous woman with the couple already married. He does not give any details about their single life or how they met, but the Bible provides many examples of courtship in that time period. Some marriages were arranged by the parents and the couple had little or no knowledge of each other. An example of this type of marriage is between Isaac and Rebekah in Genesis chapter 24.

With other marriages, the parents had little or no involvement. In Genesis chapters 28-29, Isaac sent his son Jacob to look for a wife in the land of their relatives. When he arrived, Jacob met a woman named Rachel. On his own, he asked Rachel's father for her hand. A number of years later, the couple married. During the waiting period, Jacob and Rachel probably learned a great deal about each other.

The most common marriages, however, were probably between men and women who lived in the same town and knew each other. They may have had limited social contact or they may have known each other fairly well. Their families may have been casually acquainted or they may have been close friends. Although the parents arranged the marriage, they did it with full knowledge and consent of their son or daughter.

King Lemuel does not explain how the virtuous woman gained the trust of her husband. He does not state if she had the opportunity to build trust before they were married. However, even if she gained his trust before marriage, she would need to continue building trust after they were married.

What are some ways to build trust and to break trust?

In the second part of verse 11, King Lemuel states that the husband "shall have no need of spoil." The Hebrew word translated "spoil" appears many times in the Bible. The word normally refers to wealth obtained through war or some unethical means. Since King Lemuel mentions later that the husband was a leader, he may have meant wealth that could have been acquired illegally. However, some Bible scholars believe the word in this verse refers to honest gain. In either case, one thing is clear. The husband did not need to seek additional income to please his wife and maintain his household. He truly possessed a great treasure, his wife.[1,2]

King Lemuel mentions later in the Proverb that the virtuous woman earns income through her business dealings. This income could be a reason why the husband does not need to seek spoil. However, she probably had a positive impact on the household finances in other ways as well.

List some ways that the virtuous woman may have had a positive impact on the household finances.

_____

_____

Chapter 4

A Caring Wife

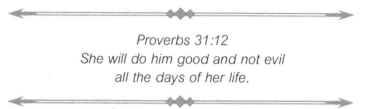

Proverbs 31:12
She will do him good and not evil
all the days of her life.

In this verse, King Lemuel may seem to be stating the obvious. However, since he brings up this point, his statement must be an important one to consider. People might assume that every wife is kind to her husband and does him no harm, but sadly wives as well as husbands say and do things to hurt each other. Sometimes, the reason is anger or frustration. Other times, the motive is revenge. Whatever the case, the root of the problem is usually a lack of love and concern for the other person.

Countless marriages have problems because wives and husbands feel that their spouse is not treating them properly. Many couples fall into destructive patterns of speech and behavior. Often, they speak to each other with sarcasm and insults. Their actions may include rude gestures or even physical confrontation. Sadly, they sometimes do more evil to each other than good.

Many women may feel like they have failed and will never be a virtuous woman because of hurtful things they have said or done. This verse, however, should not cause despair. Jesus Christ was the only person to live a perfect life on earth. Whenever we hurt someone, we need to ask forgiveness and try to undo our wrongs if possible. A virtuous woman will ask forgiveness for unkind words or actions and seek to make things right. This attitude and behavior would be one way of doing good and not evil.

List some good things a wife can do for her husband as well as some evil things she can do to him.

_____

_____

Another point to consider is the virtuous woman does good to her husband and not evil "all the days of her life." She treats him this way in good times and in bad times. She does not vacillate based on her feelings and emotions. The virtuous woman has decided to exhibit this type of behavior toward him regardless of his response. She has made a lifetime commitment to her husband and to their marriage.

Through this simple verse, King Lemuel gives a profound look into the beliefs and values of the virtuous woman. He provides many examples in this Proverb that show her heart and mind. While she may have been born with certain positive character traits, she undoubtedly needed to develop them. Some of her other good qualities, however, may not have come naturally. As a young girl, she may have displayed some bad behavior patterns. As a young bride, she may have struggled to overcome this negative behavior. The virtuous woman did not become virtuous overnight, she needed time to grow and mature like everyone.

Although this verse is about a husband and wife, the principles can be applied to relationships with family, friends, and other people.

List some good things you can do for people as well as some evil things you can do to them.

_____

_____

Chapter 5

A Willing Woman

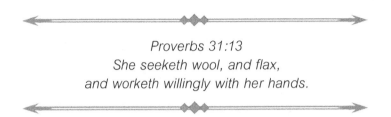

Proverbs 31:13
She seeketh wool, and flax,
and worketh willingly with her hands.

In ancient times, a significant amount of labor was required to make items of wool and linen. For wool items, the animal first had to be sheared. Then, the fleece was either thoroughly washed to remove the dirt, skin, and natural oil or lightly cleaned to remove the foreign matter but retain the oil. For linen items, the flax plants first had to be harvested. Then, the fibers needed to be extracted from the plants. Once the wool and flax fibers were obtained, they were combed to untangled them and remove any remaining particles. Next, the fibers were spun by hand into yarn. After the yarn was made, sometimes it was dyed. Finally, the wool yarn could be woven into clothes, blankets, outer garments, and other things such as tents. The flax yarn could also be woven into linen items such as clothes, sheets, curtains, and other things such as sails for ships. If the yarn had not been dyed, the entire woven item may have been dyed.[1,2,3]

The virtuous woman apparently did not own sheep or have fields of flax. The Hebrew word translated "seeketh" has the idea of inquiring and searching so she obviously went shopping for these items. King Lemuel mentions later that she worked as a seamstress and that her husband was known at the city gates so they most likely lived inside the city. Therefore, she may have gone to the city market or perhaps she visited farms. She could have purchased the items directly or bartered for them. Bartering is simply someone giving their own goods or services in exchange for the goods or services of someone else. In that time period, bartering was a common method of conducting business. If someone made a direct purchase, the person normally paid with a certain weight of a precious metal such as silver or gold since coins and printed currency did not exist.[4, 5]

The virtuous woman knew what she was seeking. She may have been trying to get the best value or she could have been looking for the best quality. Also, since wool can be different colors, she may have been seeking a certain color. If she was planning to dye the wool, she probably would have been looking for white wool. The virtuous woman obviously had a plan and was on a mission. She had done her homework and did not buy on impulse. She understood what was needed for the project and she was able to make a good decision.

What qualities does the virtuous woman display in seeking the wool and flax?

_____

_____

Although the virtuous woman had a lot of work ahead of her, she was not overwhelmed. She did not regard the work as difficult and demanding. She had a positive attitude. The Hebrew word translated "willingly" has the idea of pleasure, delight, and desire. Therefore, the virtuous woman was enthusiastic and eager as she cleaned and processed the wool and flax. She probably was excited and motivated as she thought about the finished woven items.[6]

What qualities does the virtuous woman display in preparing the wool and flax?

Wool and linen fabrics were important for ancient civilizations in this region. Wool clothing is ideal for cool weather and has some natural water repellant properties. Linen clothing is lightweight and has some natural absorption properties that make linen clothes ideal for staying comfortable in hot weather. With these two types of material, the virtuous woman was able to meet the needs of her household at both ends of the spectrum.

Chapter 6

A Providing Woman

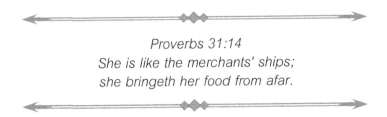

Proverbs 31:14
She is like the merchants' ships;
she bringeth her food from afar.

King Lemuel compares the virtuous woman to the ships that brought products from distant lands. To appreciate his words, we need to imagine what the arrival of these ships must have meant to people who lived thousands of years ago. In modern times, planes, trains, and motorized ships make a wide variety of products readily available. In ancient times, however, people most likely waited with great anticipation for the merchant ships to arrive. These ships sailed the seas powered only by the wind and oars. Their cargo included rare products that were greatly desired. The arrival of merchant ships must have been a time of excitement. The people probably regarded their arrival as a blessing and reason to celebrate. [1]

Similarly, the virtuous woman was a wonderful provider of food and a blessing to her household. Some of the foods may have been difficult to obtain. King Lemuel implies that she traveled long distances to get some of the items. She may have had to put down a deposit and returned later. Perhaps she had to exchange some valuable items that she owned in order to obtain the products. Nevertheless, she was able to find and acquire the foods that her household members desired.

In verse 13, the virtuous woman was seeking wool and flax to make woven items. Now, she is getting food to prepare meals for her household. The virtuous woman obviously was a knowledgeable and shrewd shopper. Often, women enjoy shopping and are good at it. They know where to get things, which places have the best prices, and who usually has them in stock. Normally, men do not like to shop and many men fail to appreciate the time and effort that goes into shopping. Yet, they often will be the first to complain when something they want is not in the home. A wise man, however, will understand the labor that is required in stocking the home and will see the woman like a merchant ship.

What qualities does the virtuous woman display in acquiring food?

Is discernment needed in shopping? Explain.

Chapter 7

A Selfless Woman

Proverbs 31:15
She riseth also while it is yet night, and giveth
meat to her household, and a portion to her maidens.

King Lemuel does not state the exact time that the virtuous woman rises but since it was still night she probably rose just before dawn. According to Jewish tradition, night was from sunset until sunrise. Some people believe this verse teaches that a woman must rise before dawn to be virtuous. However, a number of things must be considered to properly understand this verse. [1]

In that time period, the routine of the people was based around the daylight hours. Israel is located in a region where people have about twelve hours of sunlight every day of the year. After sunset, people would use candles to brighten their dark home because electric lighting did not exist. The candles provided sufficient light for them to do things such as have dinner, talk, play games, sing songs, and have family devotions. During the twelve hours of darkness, the virtuous woman and her household probably spent around four hours doing things in their home. Then, they most likely went to bed and slept about eight hours. [2]

Electric lighting has changed the daily routine for many people. With electric lights, we can mimic daylight and are no longer limited by the rising and setting of the sun. Many businesses are open 24 hours and some people work the second or third shift. At home, we can stay up late and do many activities that were difficult or impossible in ancient times.

Therefore, the emphasis of this verse should not be what time the virtuous woman rises, but what she does when she rises. Although a woman may get up early, she could squander the time. Other women may get up late for various reasons, but once they are up, they are productive. The virtuous woman arose early after a good night's sleep and started her day by serving and caring for others. She did not waste her time or spend it on herself. She deeply cared for many people and she desired to serve them.

The virtuous woman was in charge of providing meals for her household. King Lemuel already mentioned her husband and later he will mention their children. However, she may have prepared food for others as well. The Hebrew word translated as "household" could also include extended family and even servants.[3]

The word "maidens" most likely refers to her female servants. Bible scholars have debated what the virtuous woman gave them. Some believe that she gave them food. Others believe that the word "portion" refers to work and that she gave them their work assignments. She could have done both. She may have provided them food and their work assignments so they could earn wages that day. Either way, her care and concern extended to her maidens. [4,5,6]

Why do you think the virtuous woman rose early?

_____

_____

What qualities does the virtuous woman display in this verse?

_____

_____

Chapter 8

A Woman of Vision

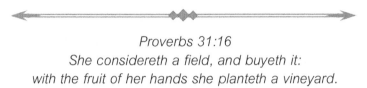

Proverbs 31:16
She considereth a field, and buyeth it:
with the fruit of her hands she planteth a vineyard.

The virtuous woman decided to take on a special project. The scope of the project involved purchasing a field and transforming the land into a vineyard. The project would be a long-term endeavor and she would have to complete a number of different phases to bring it to fruition.

King Lemuel states that the virtuous woman "considereth" which in Hebrew has the idea of thinking and imagining. She probably began by dreaming about having her own vineyard. However, the word also has the idea of devising or plotting. Therefore, she evidently planned out this project and did not rush into it or make an emotional decision. The virtuous woman had to use good judgment and plot her course. She needed to consider the risks and benefits. She had to determine a number of things such as whether the idea was practical and if the project would be financially possible. After her analysis, she decided to proceed with the first phase of the project and purchase a field.[1]

The virtuous woman may have needed to inspect a number of fields and consider many different factors. For example, she probably had to determine if the soil was good for planting and how the vineyard would be irrigated. She may have had to take into account the amount of work that would be involved in preparing the ground. She also may have needed to consider the distance of the field from her home and the travel time to go back and forth.

Although King Lemuel does not mention the cost of the field, the purchase was most likely a big investment for her. Perhaps, she was buying real estate for the first time. She may have needed to learn the legal procedures for acquiring land. She also may have had to negotiate the price and payment terms. Since she would incur expenses in other phases of the project, she had to stay within her budget.

After the virtuous woman purchased the field, she was able to begin work on the land. If the field had never been cleared, she may have had to remove rocks, bushes, and even trees. Once the ground was ready, she was able to plant her vineyard. Then, she had to devise ways to protect the crop from birds, animals, and thieves.

King Lemuel used the poetic phrase "with the fruit of her hand" to show that through her efforts and resources she planted the vineyard. The phrase also beautifully corresponds with the fruit that the vineyard would produce.

To ensure the success of the project, the virtuous woman had to consider many factors. She needed to carefully plan her steps to achieve her dream. Along the way, she may have had to make sacrifices. Nevertheless, she was able to accomplish her goal. The virtuous woman completed her vineyard project and it all started by her simply considering what could be.

What abilities does the virtuous woman display with her vineyard project?

_____

_____

What projects have you considered? Did you pursue them? Why or why not?

_____

_____

Chapter 9

A Strong Woman

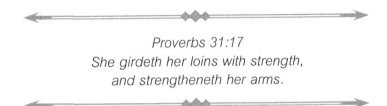

Proverbs 31:17
She girdeth her loins with strength,
and strengtheneth her arms.

King Lemuel uses figurative language in this verse which the readers of that time period would have easily understood. For modern day readers, however, the meaning of his words may not be clear. The Hebrew word translated "girdeth" usually refers to putting on or securing something such as clothing or a sword. In this case, the word refers to the virtuous woman putting on strength. The Hebrew word translated "loins" normally refers to the area around the midsection and hips. The root of this word has the idea of being slender. Therefore, the virtuous woman apparently had strong core muscles and a lean built. She no doubt became strong through hard work. [1,2]

In that time period, women performed many physically demanding tasks. One of the women's tasks was to work in the fields. The Book of Ruth states that Ruth and other women gathered the grain that the men were harvesting. King Lemuel mentioned in verse 16 that the virtuous woman purchased a field and planted a vineyard. Although she probably had helpers, she most likely was involved in clearing the field, planting, and harvesting. The stooping and bending certainly would have been a way that she strengthened her loins.

In the second part of verse 17, King Lemuel indicates that the virtuous woman also had strong arms. She was clearly a hardworking woman and had the muscles to prove it. One task that would have required her to use her arms and upper body was getting water from the town well. In the ancient Middle East, women normally were responsible for providing water for the home and the animals. Usually, the women would draw water by lowering a rope with a clay container down into the well. When the container was filled with water, they would pull it up and then carry the container on their shoulder or head to their home.[3]

As a child, the virtuous woman may have been impressed by the strength of her mother. She may have watched in amazement as her mother gracefully carried the heavy clay container filled with water. Perhaps, she playfully attempted to imitate her mother and tried to lift the container but was not able. Now, however, the virtuous woman had developed from a weak, little girl into a strong and capable woman.

Although many of her chores were physically demanding, the virtuous woman appears to have a positive attitude. The words seem to express that she wanted to be a strong woman. She probably felt a sense of pride and accomplishment in being able to complete her tasks. The virtuous woman also may have enjoyed the challenge of hard work and liked seeing the positive results it had on her body. However, her main reason for wanting to be strong was undoubtedly her desire to serve the people that she loved.

Throughout the world, people are leaving rural areas and migrating to cities. In rural areas, jobs are often hard to find, low paying, and physically demanding. In cities, jobs are often easier to find, higher paying, and less physically demanding. As a result, many people need to exercise outside of work to strengthen their bodies and maintain good health. Although differences may exist between the lifestyle of the virtuous woman and our modern lifestyle, some important principles can be drawn from her attitude and work ethic.

What do you think motivated the virtuous woman to work so hard?

_____

_____

Write down any principles from this verse that can be applied today.

_____

_____

Chapter 10

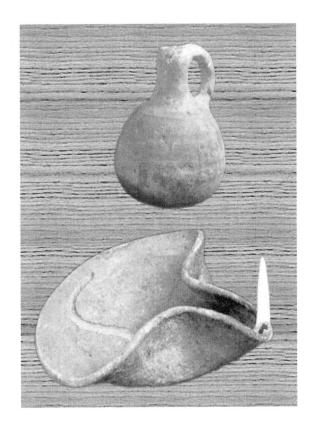

A Successful Woman

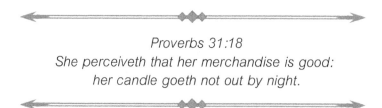

Proverbs 31:18
She perceiveth that her merchandise is good:
her candle goeth not out by night.

The virtuous woman had a valid reason for being optimistic about her merchandise. She was not relying on intuition or trusting in her feelings. She knew from experience that her merchandise was good. In Hebrew, the word translated "perceiveth" has the idea of experiencing something and the word translated "merchandise" has the idea of profit from trade. Therefore, the virtuous woman was actually selling her merchandise and earning income. She saw positive results and her optimism was based on fact.[1,2]

King Lemuel does not mention the type of merchandise that the virtuous woman sells. However, he stated in verse 16 that she planted a vineyard so she could have been selling the fruit. Also, he mentions later in verse 24 that she sells linen and girdles so her merchandise probably included these items.

The second phrase in this verse might contain the most controversial words of the entire Proverb. For many, the words "her candle goeth not out by night" generates images of an exhausted woman working all night and getting almost no sleep. However, King Lemuel does not state anywhere in this verse that the virtuous woman works all night and does not sleep.

God created our bodies with a need to sleep each day. In addition, He blessed and sanctified one day of the week as a day of rest. Sleep restores our bodies and God has worked in amazing ways throughout the Bible while people were sleeping. For example, the first time sleep is mentioned in the Bible is when God caused a deep sleep to fall upon Adam and He wonderfully created Eve. God also gave people incredible dreams and visions while they slept.

The virtuous woman surely understood that she needed to sleep and she most likely slept well each night. Without sufficient rest, she would not have been able to carry out her daily routine. At bedtime, she probably was tired because of her busy schedule and slept in peace. Her financial situation appeared to be stable and she had a good relationship with her husband and her children whom King Lemuel mentions later.

By examining the customs of this time period, we can discover a more realistic interpretation of King Lemuel's words. In our modern era of electricity, we give little thought to lighting our home. At night, we instantly have light by simply flipping a switch. Some homes even leave on an electric nightlight. In this ancient time period, however, candles were the main source of light. Their candles were different from our modern candles made of hard wax. They placed a wick in a special clay container and filled it with a fuel such as oil or animal fat. In order to have light, every home needed containers, wicks, fuel, and some type of friction tool to start the flame because matches had not yet been invented.[3,4]

Normally, the ancient civilizations of this region left a candle burning in their home throughout the night. They did this for a number of reasons. From a practical standpoint, if they needed to get up at night, they would have some light. They would not have to grope in the dark for a candle and then try to light it. In addition, a light in the home was a deterrent to thieves.

From a social point of view, a candle burning in the home at night was a positive sign. People considered the candle a symbol of prosperity and well-being. If a home did not have light at night, there was reason for concern. A dark home could have been a sign of disaster, financial ruin, or a lazy and forgetful woman.

From a religious perspective, people often believed that fire had spiritual significance. For the Jewish people, fire was especially important in their beliefs and rituals. When Moses led the Jews out of Egypt, God appeared to them at night as a pillar of fire. God also instructed Moses to make a gold candlestick that would burn continuously in the Tabernacle. In addition, God commanded Moses that the fire on the altar should never go out.

The virtuous woman probably left a candle burning for a number of reasons, but not to work all night. She was wise and conscientious so she made sure her home had containers, wicks, fuel, and friction tools. With these things, her home had light at night and her candle did not go out.[5,6]

When King Lemuel wrote this phrase, he may also have had a symbolic meaning in mind. He may have intended the candle to represent the virtuous woman. He could have been using the candle to illustrate the light that the virtuous woman provided to the home. Through her love and devotion, she was clearly a ray of light. After a busy day, she probably was tired but still had the energy and desire to spent time with the members of her household and her presence was a light to them.

Give your interpretation of the phrase "her candle goeth not out by night."

_____

_____

How can this verse be applied today? Explain.

_____

_____

Chapter 11

A Spinning Woman

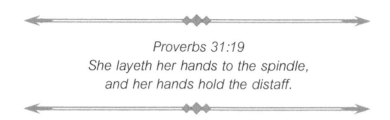

Proverbs 31:19
She layeth her hands to the spindle,
and her hands hold the distaff.

The virtuous woman used the spindle and distaff which are unfamiliar tools for many people. A person would use these tools to make yarn by hand from wool, flax, or other fibers. Usually, the spindle is a short rod for twisting the fibers together and also serves as a spool to wind the yarn around. The distaff is normally a long pole that holds the supply of fibers. Throughout the world, people still use the spindle and distaff, but spinning wheels which produce yarn much faster have widely replaced them.

Since the spindle and distaff are portable tools, the virtuous woman would have been able to make yarn without being confined to one place. She could have spun yarn while moving about her home. She also would have been able to take them with her when she went somewhere. She may have even visited a friend's house so they could spin yarn together and chat. In verse 13, the virtuous woman was seeking wool and flax. Now, she is making yarn by hand from them using these tools.

Although most women today can easily purchase yarn, some women still make their own. Many of these women use a spinning wheel, but others continue to use the spindle and distaff. Often, women enjoy spinning yarn and find it relaxing. King Lemuel does not mention if the virtuous woman enjoyed spinning yard, but she may also have found it relaxing and a way to be productive. Perhaps spinning and winding yarn helped her to relieve stress and unwind.[1]

The industrial revolution greatly changed many of the tasks that men and women had done for centuries. Factories with machinery can usually produce yarn, fabrics, and clothes cheaper and faster than making them by hand. In modern times, we lose sight of the significance of this verse and the principles that can be drawn from it.

While the way of life of the virtuous woman may have been different from our modern lifestyle, we can still learn practical lessons from her. Throughout the week, she did many different activities that show her priorities and time management. Her ultimate goal was to care and provide for her household. This verse gives us a further look into the life of the virtuous woman and a better understanding of her heart, mind, and abilities.

How do you think the virtuous woman felt about spinning yarn?

What lessons can be learned from this verse?

_____

_____

Chapter 12

A Generous Woman

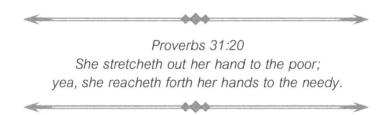

Proverbs 31:20
She stretcheth out her hand to the poor;
yea, she reacheth forth her hands to the needy.

In this verse, King Lemuel expresses the virtuous woman's concern for the poor and needy. As he wrote these words, he may have thought of his mother's words to him. In the beginning of the Proverb, his mother instructed him to help these people. He evidently listened to her counsel and embraced her teaching since he points out this quality in the virtuous woman.

As a result of her ambition, hard work, and business endeavors, the virtuous woman had the resources to help people. However, she could have felt that she worked long hours for everything that she obtained and she could have been unwilling to share with others. Yet, the virtuous woman did not respond in that way. She reached out her generous hands to help those in need.

A key theme that King Lemuel wove into the Proverb is the hands of the virtuous woman. In verse 13, he said that she worked "willingly with her hands." In verse 16, he stated that she planted a vineyard with the "fruit of her hands." He also explained in verse 19 that her "hands" used the spindle and distaff. Now, he mentions in this verse that her hands help the poor and needy.

King Lemuel used Hebrew words in these verses that specifically refer to her hands. The incredible hands of the virtuous woman worked hard not only to care for her household, but they reached out to people that she probably did not even know. Her concern was not limited to just her family and friends. The virtuous woman's kindness extended beyond her loved ones. She stretched out her compassionate hands to help those who were in need.[1]

Why do you think King Lemuel specifically mentions the hands of the virtuous woman?

Although hands do not speak, they communicate many things. Our hands express our heart and reflect our character. By our hands, we can do good or evil. The hands of the virtuous woman were strong, productive, capable, dependable, and merciful. Her hands worked eagerly to serve others. Her hands cleaned and processed the wool and flax that she diligently sought. Her hands prepared meals with the food that she brought from afar. Her hands successfully conducted business. Later in the Proverb, her hands skillfully make woven items. The amazing hands of the virtuous woman communicate loud and clear who she was and leave a wonderful legacy of her sacrificial love and service.

What legacy will you leave?

_____

_____

Chapter 13

A Confident Woman

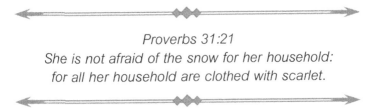

Proverbs 31:21
She is not afraid of the snow for her household:
for all her household are clothed with scarlet.

King Lemuel states a fact in this verse that is not well known. Although the climate in the Middle East is warm most of the year, the temperature can become cold during the winter and snow can fall. As the winter approached, some people might have feared that they did not have adequate clothing to keep them warm. The wardrobe of many people may have consisted only of lightweight clothing that was not suitable for the cold and snow. Warm clothing could have been considered a luxury. Therefore, the chilly days were most likely a reason for concern.

The virtuous woman, however, did not fear the cold and snow because her household had scarlet clothing. The members of her household would have included her immediate family, possibly extended family, and maybe even servants. King Lemuel does not state how many people were in her household, but he says that all of them "are clothed with scarlet."

For centuries, Bible scholars have debated the meaning of the Hebrew word translated "scarlet." Although we may never understand the exact type of clothing that King Lemuel is referring to, the people of that time period clearly understood. Obviously, the clothing was ideal for the cold and snow.

King Lemuel does not explain how the household of the virtuous woman obtained their scarlet clothing. However, he seems to imply that the virtuous woman provided the clothes. He mentions that she is not "afraid." Clearly, she was not afraid of the winter for her household had scarlet clothing, but King Lemuel might also be suggesting that she did not fear failing in her responsibility. Since he stated "her" household, the responsibility seems to be on her. One of her duties most likely was to make sure that everyone in the household had scarlet clothes in time for winter.

If the virtuous woman provided the scarlet clothes for the members of her household, she could have purchased them or made them. While King Lemuel does not say, it would seem logical that she made some or all of the scarlet clothing. Earlier in the Proverb, she was seeking wool and flax. Then, she made yarn from them using the spindle and distaff. Later in the Proverb, she makes coverings and fine linen so she definitely was a talented seamstress.

In this verse, the virtuous woman again shows her concern for the needs of her household. She obviously had to plan ahead so that they would have warm clothes in time for winter. She probably began thinking about their winter clothes long before they needed them. She may have had to start shopping early for the clothes or the material to make them. She may have had to save up silver or gold to be able to provide clothes for everyone. While other women may have been anxious and unprepared, the virtuous woman was calm and confident. She knew that she would not be frantically rushing around at the last minute trying to purchase or make warm clothing. When winter arrived, she would be ready because all of her household would be clothed in scarlet.

What qualities does the virtuous woman display in this verse?

_____

_____

Do you remember a time when you had fear of not being prepared? Explain.

_____

_____

Chapter 14

An Elegant Woman

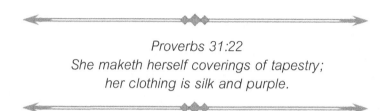

Proverbs 31:22
She maketh herself coverings of tapestry;
her clothing is silk and purple.

For centuries, people have made beautiful coverings to decorate furniture, floors, and walls. Throughout history, these coverings have been considered a luxury item because of the amount of time and skill required to make them. The oldest existing pieces of woven tapestry are from Egypt dating back to the time when the Israelites were slaves.[1,2]

The virtuous woman somehow learned the art of making these unique coverings. Although the coverings could have been part of the merchandise that King Lemuel mentioned earlier, he does not state that she sells them. He seems to indicate that they were for her own use. She probably made them to beautify her home. The reason that she might have made the coverings only for her home could have been because of the time and labor required to make them.

In the second part of verse 22, King Lemuel states that the clothing of the virtuous woman is "silk and purple." Bible scholars have debated the exact type of fabric that she wore. However, they agree that the color was purple. In the ancient Middle East, purple dye was expensive and greatly desired. Since the dye was so costly, people considered purple fabric to be luxurious. In ancient times, the royalty of various nations often dressed in purple clothing. In modern times, the royalty of some countries continue the tradition of wearing purple.[3,4]

King Lemuel's comment about the coverings and clothes provides a striking contrast to his previous description of this hardworking woman. Although she was not afraid to get her hands dirty, the virtuous woman was a woman of style and elegance. Her purple clothes were probably her dress clothes for special occasions. She most likely wore her purple clothes for religious ceremonies and social events. When she was doing her daily chores, however, she most likely wore more durable and less expensive clothing or maybe she wore her purple clothes that were old and faded.

Do you think this verse shows a different side of the virtuous woman? Explain.

_____

_____

The virtuous woman made the decorative coverings because she wanted to have a beautiful and comfortable home that she and her household could enjoy. Also, she probably wanted the home to be a place where they would be proud to invite people. In addition, she sometimes dressed in fancy clothes. Although she may have enjoyed her nice clothes and dressed this way in part for herself, her main reason was most likely that she wanted her household to be proud of her.

Chapter 15

A Supportive Wife

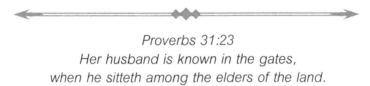

Proverbs 31:23
Her husband is known in the gates,
when he sitteth among the elders of the land.

In the ancient Middle East, many cities were encompassed by walls and had gates for entering. The area around the inside of the gates was important for a number of reasons. Usually, the city market was at this location and it was normally crowded with people. Frequently, the site was used for public discussion and debate. Kings and prophets often delivered their messages by the city gates. The elders conducted legal proceedings in this area and outside of the gates lawbreakers were punished.[1,2]

The husband of the virtuous woman held an important position. He was an influential person in the political and social affairs of their city. He was involved in the decision making of matters for the city and perhaps the region. Most people probably knew him personally or by sight. He most likely attained the position because people considered him a wise, honest, and hardworking man. In his position, he certainly must have had a lot of responsibility as well as temptations.

King Lemuel does not say if the virtuous woman had a part in her husband's fame and success. However, he seems to suggest that she did since he includes this information about her husband in a Proverb that is about her. Certainly, the husband's status in society was enhanced by the good reputation of his wife. The community surely knew that he had a responsible wife and a well-managed home.

Do you think the virtuous woman had an impact on her husband's success? Explain.

_____

_____

Earlier in the Proverb, King Lemuel mentioned that the husband trusted his wife. Since the husband was confident that his wife could manage the household and business affairs, he was able to be involved in civic affairs. While King Lemuel made it clear that the husband trusted his wife, he does not mention anywhere if the virtuous woman trusted her husband. However, he never says that she doubted him or had negative feelings toward him. She definitely understood that he was in a position of power and faced temptations from unethical men and women. Yet, she appears to trust him.

A common complaint of married men is that they feel their wife does not respect or support them. In fact, some married men feel that their wife constantly criticizes them and is actually against them. Sometimes, a wife may have good reasons for not trusting her husband. Other times, the husband may be deserving of more respect and support from his wife.

The virtuous woman and her husband seem to have built trust with each other and the community. Their marriage appears to have a solid foundation of love and respect. They apparently established a strong relationship that allowed them to accomplish many things and withstand the trials and temptations of life.

What does this verse reveal about the husband and the virtuous woman?

_____

_____

Chapter 16

A Business Woman

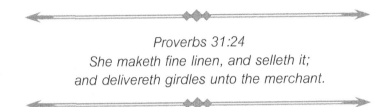

Proverbs 31:24
She maketh fine linen, and selleth it;
and delivereth girdles unto the merchant.

King Lemuel explains a little more about the product line and business of the virtuous woman in this verse. He mentions two specific items, fine linen and girdles. The Hebrew word translated "fine linen" has the idea of linen material used for clothing. The virtuous woman could have sold just linen material or she could have tailored it into garments.[1]

The girdles that the virtuous woman supplied to the merchant were most likely linen as well. Since linen girdles were more expensive than the more common leather girdles, her profit margins would have been higher. In the ancient Middle East, both men and women wore girdles as part of their regular dress. The girdles were worn on top of clothing and used as a belt. People tightened their robes with their girdle and used them to hold or hang things. Often, women would use them as a purse and men would hang their sword on their girdle.[2]

The virtuous woman appears to have sold her fine linen to the general public but she had a special agreement with the merchant for the girdles. The Hebrew word translated "merchant" refers to the Canaanite people who were well known as traders. The Canaanites had established extensive trade routes by land and sea. They must have liked the price and quality of the girdles that the virtuous woman was selling. She also must have provided them with fast and reliable delivery.[3, 4, 5]

The virtuous woman apparently established herself as a respected supplier of fine linen and girdles. Her sales of girdles to the Canaanite merchant community most likely increased her production demands. As a result, she may have been able to provide work for family, servants, and even people in the community.

King Lemuel does not explain how the virtuous woman learned to conduct business. He gives no information about her educational or work background. Perhaps her mother had a business and as a young girl she helped her and observed her methods. Maybe her father or another relative had a business where she worked and gained experience. Possibly, her husband taught her about doing business. However, another possibility is that she had no example or mentor. She may have learned everything on her own by trial and error. Whatever the case, the virtuous woman gained the knowledge and developed the skills that she needed to successfully produce and sell her merchandise. Through her business relationship with the merchant, her products were now probably reaching distant lands.

What abilities does the virtuous woman display in this verse?

_____

_____

Chapter 17

An Esteemed Woman

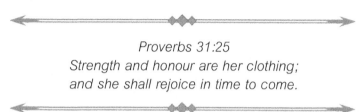

Proverbs 31:25
Strength and honour are her clothing;
and she shall rejoice in time to come.

King Lemuel mentions the clothing of the virtuous woman again in this verse, but his words this time are figurative. His words refer to her and not the garments that she is wearing. He uses the clothing to portray an image of her character. He chose two key words as symbols to represent her. Through these words, he communicates the type of woman that she is.

The first word that King Lemuel chose was "Strength" which he used in verse 17 to describe her physical condition. Although he used the same Hebrew word in this verse, he most likely meant something more than just muscles. The word can refer to many types of strength. Therefore, he may have been referring to such things as her mental, emotional, or spiritual strength. The virtuous woman was truly a woman of inner strength as well as physical strength.[1]

The second word that he chose was "honour." The virtuous woman had a good name and a good reputation. She was the wife of a prominent man, a respected businesswoman, and a capable homemaker. King Lemuel also indicates later that she had the love and respect of her children and husband. The virtuous woman had achieved many things in life and had attained a place of status in society.

Write your thoughts on the meaning of the clothing of the virtuous woman.

_____

_____

In the second part of verse 25, King Lemuel states that the virtuous woman was able to rejoice in the time to come. People often struggle to rejoice for many different reasons. Sometimes things happen that we have no control over that cause us grief and hardship. Other times, we bring on our own problems and sorrows because of bad decisions.

What do you think are some of the reasons the virtuous woman could rejoice?

_____

_____

The virtuous woman lived life to the fullest. She made the most of every day and did not waste her time. She did not grumble or complain about the work that she had to do. The virtuous woman enjoyed serving others and did things out of love, not obligation. She made wise decisions and choices. She built a strong foundation in her public and private life. She planned and prepared for the future. As a result, the virtuous woman had a positive outlook and she could rejoice in the days ahead.

Chapter 18

A Wise Woman

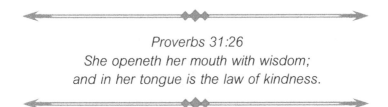

Proverbs 31:26
She openeth her mouth with wisdom;
and in her tongue is the law of kindness.

The mother of King Lemuel told her son in verse 9 that he should open his mouth and judge righteously. Similarly, King Lemuel states in this verse that the virtuous woman "openeth her mouth with wisdom." He uses the same Hebrew word for open which has the idea of opening wide. Therefore, he seems to be emphasizing that the virtuous woman spoke up and shared wise counsel. He most likely is not referring to public speaking, but rather her conversations with family, friends, and others.[1]

In the second part of verse 26, King Lemuel mentions the "tongue" of the virtuous woman. He says that in it is "the law of kindness." The word "law" could be referring to her own principles and values. However, the word in Hebrew is "torah" which often refers to the law of God. Therefore, King Lemuel may have used this word to convey the idea that she knew God's law and that her thoughts and speech were influenced by it.[2]

The wise counsel of the virtuous woman most likely included words of correction. However, she appears to have spoken them with compassion since King Lemuel includes the word "kindness." The virtuous woman obviously understood the powerful impact that words can have on people. She must have chosen her words carefully and did not speak impulsively.

King Lemuel does not mention any listening skills of the virtuous woman, but she had to be a good listener. An important part of being a good communicator is listening to others. She must have paid attention to what others were saying so she could respond to them appropriately. However, the virtuous woman surely did not listen to gossip since she was a woman of honor and integrity. She certainly knew that foolish talk could spread rumors and hurt others. She most likely had a gentle and tactful way of turning the conversation in a positive direction.

What are some ways that the virtuous woman could have learned to speak with wisdom?

The virtuous woman excelled in many areas of life, but perhaps the most important area was communicating with others. Words can encourage or discourage. Words can unite or divide. Words can bring peace or stir up strife. Words can contain wisdom or folly. The virtuous woman mastered the art of verbal communication and spoke to people with wisdom and kindness. Her words contained love and sound judgment. She provides an excellent example of how to speak with others.

How can you improve your communications skills?

_____

_____

Chapter 19

A Watchful Woman

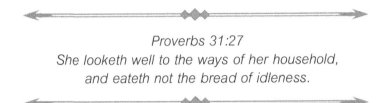

Proverbs 31:27
She looketh well to the ways of her household,
and eateth not the bread of idleness.

Watchmen played an important role in the ancient Middle East. They looked out for various threats and concerns. Cities usually had a watchman to alert the people when enemies were approaching. Farmers often had a watchman to protect their crops from thieves and animals. The Jewish people even considered prophets to be watchmen who warned the people about straying from the Lord.[1]

In this verse, King Lemuel used a Hebrew word translated as "looketh well" which has the idea of keeping watch. In other passages of the Bible, the same word is actually translated as "watchman." The word indicates that the virtuous woman looked out for her household. Since men were usually watchmen for physical dangers, she most likely watched for other problems.[2]

The word "ways" in Hebrew has the idea of people walking together. Therefore, King Lemuel is saying that the virtuous woman observed the ways of the people in her household. Each person had their own personality and temperament. Their behavior had either a positive or negative effect on others. As they journeyed together through life, the virtuous woman kept a close watch for problems that could cause division.[3]

In addition, the virtuous woman surely looked at the affect society was having on the members of her household. She no doubt attempted to teach good values but understood that others outside of the home were sending different messages. Therefore, she probably kept an eye on the direction of their lives to make sure they were on the right path.

The greatest failure of a watchman is to neglect his job and be unaware when the enemy comes. King Lemuel uses an illustration to show that the virtuous woman did not neglect her job. He says that she "eateth not the bread of idleness." The illustration emphasizes that the virtuous woman was not lazy but active and faithful in her surveillance of the household.

The virtuous woman supplied not only material needs for the household but she also kept a watchful eye on all of the members. She was concerned for their physical and emotional health. She loved and cared for the whole person. She truly was a good watchman or maybe more accurately stated a good watchwoman.

What are some characteristics of a good watchman?

Do you have responsibilities as a watchman for your family or friends? Explain.

_____

_____

Chapter 20

A Blessed Woman

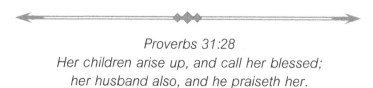

Proverbs 31:28
Her children arise up, and call her blessed;
her husband also, and he praiseth her.

In the first part of this verse, King Lemuel mentions the children of the virtuous woman. He does not state their ages, but they would seem to be younger children. He says that they "arise up" which may refer to them standing to show honor and respect to their mother. He also says that they "call her blessed." Their compliment would be uncommon for younger children. Although young children may admire their mother, they rarely express it. Often, they do not know how to put their feelings into words. Also, they normally take things for granted and do not appreciate their mother until they are older. The virtuous woman's children, however, compliment her. Their communication and conduct are impressive. They acknowledge their mother by their speech as well as their posture.[1]

Write your thoughts on the communication and conduct of the virtuous woman's children.

_____

_____

The comment of King Lemuel shows at least two things. First, the children genuinely loved and admired their mother. Second, they had good education in the home since they behaved and spoke in this manner. Their behavior and speech are a testimony to the teaching and example of their mother and father. The virtuous woman and her husband obviously taught their children to talk to people with honor and respect. Although King Lemuel writes only a few words in this verse, he speaks volumes. With these brief words, he provides an insightful glimpse into the home life of the virtuous woman.

How can parents teach their children to speak to others with respect?

_____

_____

In the second part of verse 28, King Lemuel mentions the virtuous woman's husband. He stated earlier that the husband was a leader so he could have been a good communicator. However, he also could have been the strong, silent type. He may have been like many men who have trouble expressing their feelings. King Lemuel does not say whether the husband was a good communicator but he does mention that the husband praises his wife. The husband's exact words are stated in verse 29 and will be discussed in the following chapter.

Some people might expect children to speak well of their mother and a husband to speak well of his wife. Family members, however, can sometimes be our biggest critics and quick to point out faults. Good relationships within the family are not always easy to maintain. While the family should be a source of encouragement and support, this is often not the case. The virtuous woman had a positive impact on her family. She gained their love and respect and they praised her.

What are some ways you can encourage family members?

_____

_____

Chapter 21

A Special Woman

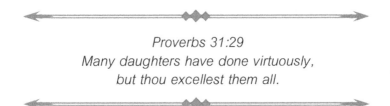

Proverbs 31:29
Many daughters have done virtuously,
but thou excellest them all.

King Lemuel makes known the husband's words of praise to his wife in this verse. Although the husband does not say much, his words are genuine and sincere. Sadly, some men are smooth talkers and use words to deceive and manipulate women. The husband, however, is truly thankful for his wife and expresses his love and gratitude to her. His compliment is a wonderful testimony of his admiration for his wife. His words probably made her feel like the most special woman in the world.

Men and women often say that no woman could ever compare to the woman in this Proverb and this verse probably confirms that idea for them. However, King Lemuel wants to encourage men to seek a wife like this woman so he is not teaching that men will never find one like her. Also, he wants to encourage women to be like this woman so he certainly is not suggesting that women will never measure up to her.

The words in this verse are a compliment that the husband gives to his wife. The compliment is meant to show his wife how much he thinks of her and not intended to put down other women. His compliment could be compared to compliments that other men might give to their wife. For example, a husband might say to his wife that she is the best cook in the world. The wife certainly would appreciate his words and feel honored although she obviously knows that there are many good cooks in the world. Another husband might say to his wife that she is the most beautiful woman on earth. The wife most likely would feel flattered and know his intention is to make her feel special, but she no doubt understands there are many beautiful women. Similarly, the virtuous woman must have cherished her husband's words. However, she surely knew that there were other women that were virtuous and worthy of praise.

How would you interpret the husband's comment?

King Lemuel intended this Proverb to be a source of inspiration, not discouragement. In the Proverb, he describes qualities that most likely he and his mother had observed. All women, whether single or married, with children or without children, have the potential to be like this woman. Some women may already be like her. Others may need to grow in certain areas of their life. Other women, however, might need to make significant changes in their speech, actions, and attitudes. Regardless of the situation, God is able to transform lives. With Him, all things are possible.

Do you think all women can be like the virtuous woman? Explain.

_____

_____

Chapter 22

A Beautiful Woman

Proverbs 31:30
Favour is deceitful, and beauty is vain:
but a woman that feareth the Lord, she shall be praised.

Some women are born with incredible, physical beauty. One beautiful woman mentioned in the Bible was Queen Esther and her amazing story is recorded in the Book of Esther. Many women long to have a beautiful appearance, but they were not endowed with the natural features possessed by women like Queen Esther. Therefore, they often turn to cosmetics in order to fulfill this desire. Charles Revson, the founder of the Revlon cosmetic company, said "we sell hope." He obviously meant that through their beauty products they provide women that were not born with the looks of Queen Esther the hope of being visually beautiful.[1]

In this verse, King Lemuel also provides hope to women. However, he offers a different kind of hope. He gives women the hope that they can be spiritually beautiful and this type of beauty is truly worthy of praise. Physical beauty is vain since it does not last and favor is deceitful because it can be lost, but spiritual beauty is something that endures.

The Hebrew word translated "feareth" has the idea of reverence. A woman that fears the Lord will seek to honor and serve Him. Her devotion to God will overflow into genuine love and concern for people as well. King Lemuel wants men and women to recognize and appreciate a woman that fears the Lord. He wants us to realize that she has an incorruptible beauty that should be praised.[2]

King Lemuel does not give a physical description of the virtuous woman except that she had a strong upper and lower body. He does not mention whether she had a pretty face or an impressive figure. She may have been physically attractive or she could have been a plain woman. However, King Lemuel indicates that the virtuous woman had spiritual beauty. All women may not be physically beautiful like Queen Esther, but all women can be spiritually beautiful like the virtuous woman in this Proverb.

One of the main teachings in the book of Proverbs is to obtain wisdom. Men and women need to learn to look beyond the physical and have spiritual discernment. We need to perceive life through spiritual eyes and esteem the things that are truly worthy of praise.

What importance do most men place on a woman's physical and spiritual beauty?

_____

_____

_____

_____

What importance do most women place on their own physical and spiritual beauty?

Chapter 23

A Deserving Woman

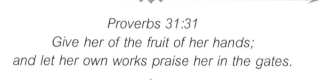

Proverbs 31:31
Give her of the fruit of her hands;
and let her own works praise her in the gates.

King Lemuel ends the Proverb in a truly surprising and unexpected way. He dramatically concludes his teaching on the virtuous woman by issuing a royal decree. However, the command is something that probably no one was anticipating. After describing the character and qualities of this virtuous woman, he does not command other women to be like her. Instead, he commands people to treat her properly. His closing statement provides not only words of wisdom, but a mandate that people are to heed and obey.

Throughout the Proverb, King Lemuel commented on the amazing hands of the virtuous woman that touched the lives of many people. Now, he declares, "Give her of the fruit of her hands." The word "Give" in Hebrew is in the imperative form which indicates the phrase is a command. The word has the idea of ascribing or bestowing. Therefore, King Lemuel is commanding people to give the virtuous woman the recognition that she deserves. Often, women are not appreciated and the work done by women is not valued. King Lemuel's command is meant to ensure that the virtuous woman receives the credit and honor for all the things that she has done. [1,2]

In addition, this Hebrew word has the idea of giving something material. Therefore, the command of King Lemuel probably includes properly compensating the virtuous woman. Maybe some of her customers were taking advantage of her kindness and not paying their bills. Perhaps the merchants were exploiting her because she was a woman. Possibly, her husband managed the household income and he was not aware of the financial needs of his wife. Whatever the case, King Lemuel is looking out for the virtuous woman.[3]

When men and women read this Proverb, they often overlook King Lemuel's command and focus on what a woman should do to be virtuous. Although King Lemuel teaches about the virtuous woman, his only command in the Proverb is for people to treat her fairly and respectfully. His command certainly is intended not only for this woman, but all virtuous women who sacrificially serve others. In addition, the command could be applied in general to all women no matter where they are on the path to becoming a virtuous woman.

What are some ways to obey King Lemuel's command?

People often criticize the Bible because they say that it puts down women. They believe that the Bible was written by chauvinistic men who did not respect women. However, this verse proves otherwise. In this ancient Bible Proverb, King Lemuel boldly stands up for women's rights.

One of the reasons that King Lemuel wrote this Proverb was to encourage women and give them hope. His reference to "the gates" has the idea of public praise because the area around the city gates was usually a busy place full of people and chatter. Therefore, he is declaring that her accomplishments be publicly acknowledged and praised. The Jewish people have correctly understood this Proverb. As mentioned in Chapter 1, they have sung these verses for generations as a way to praise and honor women.

The Proverb began with the mother of King Lemuel teaching her son. As stated earlier in Chapter 1, the word "taught" in Hebrew has the idea of both instruction and correction. We do not know when his mother first began to teach him. She may have begun by tenderly telling him bedtime stories when he was a child. Then, she could have patiently counseled him when he was a teenager. Later, she may have had to lovingly confront him when he was a young man going down the wrong path. Although we cannot be sure of King Lemuel's reaction to his mother's words when he was young, he ultimately made them his own. This Proverb is a wonderful testimony that the words of a mother to her child were heard and remembered!

Through this Proverb, King Lemuel teaches both men and women, as his mother taught him, to esteem the qualities possessed by the virtuous woman. He also commands people to give her everything that she deserves. In addition, King Lemuel encourages women to be the women that God wants them to be. Some women spend their time looking for love in all the wrong places. The virtuous woman loved and served in the place where she was. She bloomed where she was planted. She worked diligently, shared generously, and loved unconditionally. King Lemuel understood the value of a virtuous woman and strove to teach the world that she is precious!

If you enjoyed this Bible study,
please recommend it to your friends.
Also, we would very much appreciate your positive
feedback on social media and book review sites.
If you would like more information on a personal
relationship with God, please contact us.

Abidan

Publishers of Educational and Inspirational Books

www.abidanbooks.com

Bibliography

Chapter 1

1. H3256 yacar, *Strong's Hebrew Lexicon*. Blue Letter Bible. www.blueletterbible.org//lang/lexicon/lexicon.cfm?Strongs=H3256&t=KJV
2. Waltke, Bruce K. *The book of Proverbs: 2, chapters 15-31*, Grand Rapids, MI: William B. Eerdmans Pub., 2005, pp.501-536
3. *"Eishet Chayil – A Song for Friday Night"* Aleph Beta, Hoffberger Institute for Text Study, Inc. www.alephbeta.org/shabbat/eshet-proverbs-31-meaning-explained

Chapter 2

1. H2428 chayil, *Strong's Hebrew Lexicon*. Blue Letter Bible. www.blueletterbible.org//lang/lexicon/lexicon.cfm?Strongs=H2428&t=KJV
2. Harris, Laird R., Archer, Gleason L. Jr., Waltke, Bruce K. *Theological Wordbook of the Old Testament*. Chicago: Moody Press, 1980, pp. 271-272
3. Botterweck, Johannes, G. Ringgren, Helmer, *Theological Dictionary of the Old Testament*, Vol. 4, Grand Rapids, MI: William B. Eerdmans Publishing Co., 1981, pp 348-358

Chapter 3

1. H7998 – shalal, *Strong's Hebrew Lexicon*. Blue Letter Bible. www.blueletterbible.org//lang/lexicon/lexicon.cfm?Strongs=H7998&t=KJV
2. Jamieson, Robert. Fausset A.R, & Brown, David. *Commentary on the Whole Bible*, Online, Proverbs 31 www.ccel.org/ccel/jamieson/jfb/jfb.x.xx.xxxii.html

Chapter 5

1. *Textile Manufacturing*, New World Encyclopedia, www.newworldencyclopedia.org/entry/Textile_manufacturing
2. *Linen*, Biblical Training, www.biblicaltraining.org/library/linen
3. Youngblood, Ronald F., Harrison, R. K., Bruce, F. F. *Nelson's Illustrated Bible Dictionary: New and Enhanced Edition*, Nashville, TN : Thomas Nelson, 2014, pp. 254-255.

4. H1875 – darash, *Strong's Hebrew Lexicon*. Blue Letter Bible.
www.blueletterbible.org//lang/lexicon/lexicon.cfm?strongs=H1875&t=KJV

5. Brand, Chad, Mitchell, Eric. *Holman Illustrated Bible Dictionary, Revised and Expanded*, Nashville, TN: B&H, 2015 pp.314-315

6. Unger, Merrill F., Vine W. E. *Vine's Complete Expository Dictionary of Old and New Testament Words: With Topical Index*, "Pleasure" E-Book, Nashville, TN: Thomas Nelson, 1996

Chapter 6

1. *Antique Ships*, Naval Encyclopedia,
www.naval-encyclopedia.com/antique-ships

Chapter 7

1. *Day And Night*, Jewish Virtual Library,
www.jewishvirtuallibrary.org/day-and-night

2. *Duration of Daylight/Darkness Table for One Year*, The United States Naval Observatory.
aa.usno.navy.mil/data/docs/Dur_OneYear.php

3. Botterweck, Johannes, G. Ringgren, Helmer. *Theological Dictionary of the Old Testament*, Vol. 5, Grand Rapids, MI: William B. Eerdmans Publishing Co., 1986, p. 348

4. Delitzsch, Franz. *Biblical Commentary on the Proverbs of Solomon*, Ediburg, Scottland, T & T Clark, 1884 pp. 329-330
archive.org/stream/BiblicalCommentaryOldTestament.KeilAndDelitzsch.6/0
4.BCOT.KD.PoeticalBooks.vol.4.Writings.#page/n1355

5. Hubbard, David A. *The Preacher's Commentary*, Vol. 15: Proverbs, Nashville, TN: Thomas Nelson, 2004, p. 480

6. Clarke, Adam. *The Holy Bible With A Commentary And Critical Notes*, New York: G Lane & P.P. Sandford, 1843, p. 792,
archive.org/details/ClarkeBible03/page/n799

Chapter 8

1. H2161 – zamam, *Strong's Hebrew Lexicon*. Blue Letter Bible,
www.blueletterbible.org//lang/lexicon/lexicon.cfm?Strongs=H2161&t=KJV

Chapter 9

1. H2296 – chagar, *Strong's Hebrew Lexicon*. Blue Letter Bible, www.blueletterbible.org//lang/lexicon/lexicon.cfm?Strongs=H2296&t=KJV
2. Brand, Chad, Mitchell, Eric. *Holman Illustrated Bible Dictionary, Revised and Expanded*, Nashville, TN: B&H, 2015 p.1024
3. Orr, James. *International Standard Bible Encyclopedia*, Volume II, Chicago: The Howard-Severance Co., 1915, pp.873-874

Chapter 10

1. Brown, Francis, Driver. S. R., Briggs, Charles A. *A Hebrew and English lexicon of Old Testament: with an appendix containing the biblical Aramaic*, Oxford: Clarendon Press, 1906, p. 381
2. H5504 – cachar, *Strong's Hebrew Lexicon*. Blue Letter Bible, www.blueletterbible.org//lang/lexicon/lexicon.cfm?Strongs=H5504&t=KJV
3. Untitled article on the history of candles, National Candle Association. Washington, DC.
www.candles.org/history
4. Goren-Inbar, N., Freikman, M., Garfinkel, Y., Goring-Morris, N.A., Grosman, L. "*The Earliest Matches*." PLoS ONE 7(8): e42213
journals.plos.org/plosone/article?id=10.1371/journal.pone.0042213
5. Orr, James. *International Standard Bible Encyclopedia*, Volume II Chicago: The Howard-Severance Co., 1915, pp.1825-1826
6. Douglas, J. D., Tenney, Merrill C., Silva, Moises. *Zondervan Illustrated Bible Dictionary*, Grand Rapids, MI: Zondervan, 2011, pp.829, 1163

Chapter 11

1. Amos, Alden. *The Alden Amos Big Book of Handspinning: Being A Compendium of Information, Advice, and Opinions On the Noble Art & Craft*, Loveland, CO: Interweave Press, 2001

Chapter 12

Perowne, J. J. Stewart. *The Cambridge Bible for schools and colleges*, Cambridge: At The University Press, 1899, p.191

Chapter 14
1. Clarke, Adam. *The Adam Clarke Commentary*, Online, Proverbs 7 and 31
https://beta.studylight.org/commentaries/acc/proverbs-7.html.
https://beta.studylight.org/commentaries/eng/acc/proverbs-31.html
2. Jarry, Madeleine. "Tapestry" *Encycloaedia Britannica*, Encyclopaedia Britannica, Inc. August 02, 2013
www.britannica.com/art/tapestry
3. Cardon, Dominique. *Natural Dyes, Sources, Traditions, Technology and Science*, London: Archetype Publications, 2007, pp. 553-606
4. Freedman, David Noel. *The Anchor Bible Dictionary*, New York: Doubleday, 1992, pp. 557-559

Chapter 15
1. Freedman, David Noel. *Eerdmans Dictionary of the Bible*, Grand Rapids, MI: William B. Eerdmans Publishing Company, 2000, p.483-484
2. Mark, Joshua J. "Wall" *Ancient History Encyclopedia*, 02 Sep 2009
www.ancient.eu/wall/

Chapter 16
1. H5466 – cadiyn, *Strong's Hebrew Lexicon*, Blue Letter Bible,
www.blueletterbible.org//lang/lexicon/lexicon.cfm?Strongs=H5466&t=KJV
2. Smith, William. *Dr. William Smith's Dictionary of the Bible: comprising its antiquities, biography, geography, and natural history*, Volume 2, New York: Hurd and Houghtn, Cambridge: Riverside Press, 1872 pp. 928-929
3. H3669 - Kĕna`aniy, *Strong's Hebrew Lexicon*, Blue Letter Bible,
www.blueletterbible.org//lang/lexicon/lexicon.cfm?Strongs=H3669&t=KJV
4. Niels, Peter Lemche. *The Canaanites and Their Land: The Tradition of the Canaanites*, Sheffield: JSOT Press, 1999, pp. 123-150
5. Cartwright, Mark. *Trade in the Phoenician World*, Ancient History Encyclopedia, 01 Apr 2016.
www.ancient.eu/article/881/trade-in-the-phoenician-world/

Chapter 17
1. Brown, Francis, Driver. S. R., Briggs, Charles A. *A Hebrew and English lexicon of Old Testament: with an appendix containing the biblical Aramaic*, Oxford: Clarendon Press, 1906, pp. 738-739

Chapter 18
1. H6605 – towrah, Strong's Hebrew Lexicon, Blue Letter Bible, www.blueletterbible.org/lang/lexicon/lexicon.cfm?strongs=H6605&t=KJV
2. H8451 – towrah, Strong's Hebrew Lexicon, Blue Letter Bible, www.blueletterbible.org//lang/lexicon/lexicon.cfm?strongs=H8451&t=KJV

Chapter 19
1. Douglas, J. D., Tenney, Merrill C., Silva, Moises. *Zondervan Illustrated Bible Dictionary*, "Watchman" E-Book, Grand Rapids, MI: Zondervan, 2009
2. H6822 - tsaphah - *Strong's Hebrew Lexicon*, Blue Letter Bible, www.blueletterbible.org//lang/lexicon/lexicon.cfm?strongs=H6822&t=KJV
3. H1979 – haliykah, *Strong's Hebrew Lexicon*, Blue Letter Bible. www.blueletterbible.org//lang/lexicon/lexicon.cfm?strongs=H1979&t=KJV

Chapter 20
1. Hubbard, David A. *The Communicator's Commentary*, Dallas, TX.: Word Books, 1989, p484

Chapter 22
1. Revson, Charles. *"Legacy"* Revlon, www.revlon.com/behind-the-color/legacy
2. Unger, Merrill F. Vine W. E. *Vine's Complete Expository Dictionary of Old and New Testament Words: With Topical Index*, "To Fear yare' (3372)" E-Book, Nashville, TN: Thomas Nelson, 1996

Chapter 23
1. Hubbard, David A. The Preacher's Commentary Vol. 15: Proverbs, Nashville, TN : Thomas Nelson, 2004, p. 484
2. H5414 - nathan - *Strong's Hebrew Lexicon*, Blue Letter Bible, www.blueletterbible.org//lang/lexicon/lexicon.cfm?strongs=H5414&t=KJV

3. Fox, Michael V. Proverbs 10-31, New Haven, CT, Yale University Press, 2009, p. 899

Image Credits

Cover
Crown created from adapted images:
Neliubov, Iaroslav. © 123RF.com
Crocker, Casey. *Crater of Diamonds 2.63 White Diamond*, Arkansas Department of Parks, Heritage and Tourism, 2018
Astynax, *Virgin Valley Black Opal*, 2009
Daughtry, Claudia. *Onyx Stone, Jasper Stone, Carnelian Stone*, 2020

Chapter 1
Tillack, Johannes Adolf. Rachel and Little Joseph, Date Unknown

Chapter 2
Artist Unknown. Untitled, Adapted Drawing , David C. Cook Publishing, Card, 1828

Chapter 3
Stemler, O. A. and Cleveland, Bess Bruce, Naaman goes to Israel for healing from leprosy, Standard Bible Reader, Three, 1926

Chapter 4
Bondoux, J. Geoges. *La Sulamite*, Date Unknown

Chapter 5
Tissot J. James. *Ruth Takes Away The Barley*, 1904, The Old Testament: Three Hundred and Ninety-six Compositions Illustrating the Old Testament

Chapter 6
Macaulay James. *A Phenician Galley*, 1880, Sea Pictures Drawn in Pen and Pencil

Chapter 7
Jebulon. Adapted Digital Photograph, Pottery kiln, 2016,
Archaeological Museum of Eretria, PD-Release
Vernet Lecomte, Emile. Adapted Drawing of *Maronites à la fontaine*,
1863, PD-US
Adapted Digital Photograph, of *Beveled rim bowl. Clay, from
Nineveh, Late Uruk Period, 3300-3100 BC*. British Museum

Chapter 8
Elphick, Fred. Adapted Drawing of *Ruth resting in the harvest field
noticed by Boaz*, 1911.
יעקב, Adapted photo of *Barren Field* in Israel, 2007, PD-Release.

Chapter 9
Cabanel, Alexander. *Young Beauty, 1800's*

Chapter 10
Nightingale, Ross. Adapted Digital Photograph of *Judean Oil Lamp
and Iron Age Oil Juglet*, Bibleworld Museum & Discovery Centre,
New Zealand. www.windowintothebible.com/everyday-lamps

Chapter 11
Lenoir, Charles-Amable. *The Spinner by the Sea*, 1800's –1900's

Chapter 12
Artist Unknown. Adapted Drawing of *The Good Wife*, Castle and
Company, 1800's

Chapter 13
Stemler, O. A. and Cleveland, Bess Bruce. Adapted Untitled
Drawing, Standard Bible Reader Two, 1925

Chapter 14
Bridgman, Frederick Arthur. Adapted Painting of *Dans Une Ville de
Campagne Alger*, 1888

Chapter 15
Artist Unknown. *He Drew Off His Sandal And Handed It To Boaz*,
The Farmer Boy The Story Of Jacob, Henry Altemus Company,
1905

Chapter 16
Fabbi, Fabio. *Choosing the silk*, 1900's

Chapter 17
Merle, Hugues Georges. *A Turkish Beauty*, 1868

Chapter 18
Artist Unknown. Untitled, The Bible in Picture and Story by
Louise Seymour Houghton, American Tract Society, 1889

Chapter 19
Wontner, William Clarke. *Safie*, 1900

Chapter 20
Stacey, Walter Sydney. Untitled, 1910

Chapter 21
Bridgman, Frederick Arthur. Le Deuxieme Tete a Tete, 1880

Chapter 22
Artist Unknown. Adapted Drawing of *Hannah Praying In The
Lord's House*, The Child's Bible, Cassell, Petter, Galpin & Co. 1883

Chapter 23
Tissot, James. Adapted Painting of The Resurrection of the
Widow's Son at Nain,1800's
Artist Initials EJH. Adapted Drawing of Rebekah, Castle &
Company, 1852

Made in the USA
Coppell, TX
06 July 2021